BLAZON

Michael Bobb

BLAZON

With framed colour pictures

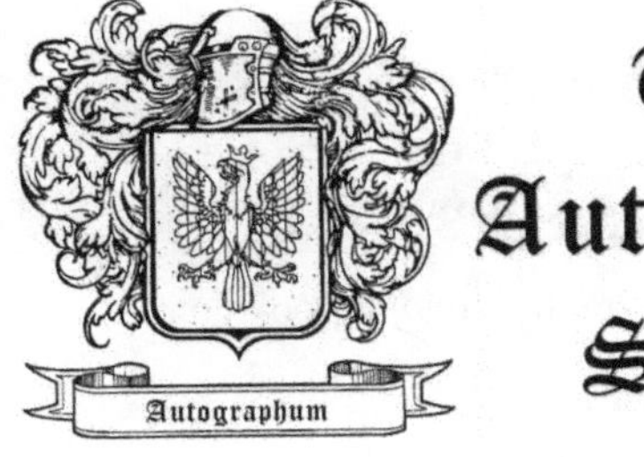

The
Autograph
Score

First published in 2023
by The Autograph Score
www.theautographscore.co.uk

11

Paperback
ISBN 978-1-7392947-4-8

E-book
ISBN 978-1-7392947-5-5

The Autograph Score - London
theautographscore@outlook.com

"The crown of literature is poetry. It is
the end and aim. It is the sublimest
activity of the human mind. It is the
achievement of beauty."

W. Somerset Maugham
Cakes and Ale

TABLE OF CONTENTS

LIST OF PLATES

INTRODUCTION

Coat of Arms where developed in the Middle Ages as a means of identifying warriors in battle and tournaments. These colourful identification designs were displayed with great pride. Records were kept that gave each knight exclusive rights to his Arms. In many cases, records were compiled listing the family name and an exact description of the Coat of Arms. These are called 'armorials' or 'blazons'. The word 'heraldry' is associated with Coat of Arms. This is due to the role of the 'herald' in recording a blazon, ensuring that a family maintained its protective rights to have and use its individual Arms.

It is important to note that the word blazon is the correct technical description for a Coat of Arms. The blazon gives a description of the charge. Almost anything that can be symbolised in colour or form can be a charge. Charges include representations of animals, people, monsters, divine beings, natural and man-made objects. An eagle looking over its right shoulder and with its talons and wings outstretched is called 'displayed', as seen on the front cover of this book.

Colours used in heraldry represents a clue about the bearer. Gold or yellow denotes generosity, valour or perseverance. Silver or white represents serenity and nobility. The other colours are red, green, black, blue and purple. Red represents fortitude and creative power. Green means hope, vitality and plenty. Black is for repentance or Vengeance. Blue and purple represent loyalty and splendour.

The furs most commonly used are Ermine and Vair. Ermine represents dignity and nobility; Vair, a high mark of dignity.

The present function of the Coat of Arms, although still one of identity, serves more to preserve the traditions that arose from its earlier use.

The Bobb Coat of Arms is officially documented in <u>Cadena's Repertorio de Blasones de la Comunidad Hispanica.</u> The original description of the Arms, or Shield, is:

"EN ORO, UN ÁGUILA, DE GULES, CORONADA."

When translated the blazon also describes the original colours of the Bobb Arms as:

"Gold; a red eagle, crowned."

"In the beginning was the Word, and the Word was with God, and the Word was God."

John
chapter 1, verse 1
KJV

The Blazon And The Sword

Hurrah, hurrah!
Three cheers for the king
On horseback he marches
Hurrah, for the king!

He marches high
Formidable and strong
Trailing behind
A captured throng

Ahead are the knights
Thrashing the way
In middle-time forest
Clearing the way

Great, conquering king
Blazon quiet in the hand
Sword in the right
Restrains not the command

Fairest of all maidens
Crown an auburn glow
Holds lace etched sword
Gauntlet of mistletoe

She gazes from tower
High on forest's hill
And sees the cavalcade
An approaching still

She whispers to the wind
A comely dove lands on
Her outstretched arm
Just lower than the sun

She whispers to the dove
The dove flies to the king
Flying high, flying low
Melodies the offering

The dove sings of secrets
Only pure doves understand
Flying high, flying low
Obeying the king's right hand

The dove lands on the blazon
Soft thunder, yes, echoes
Breaks the hard chains
Of captives behind, below

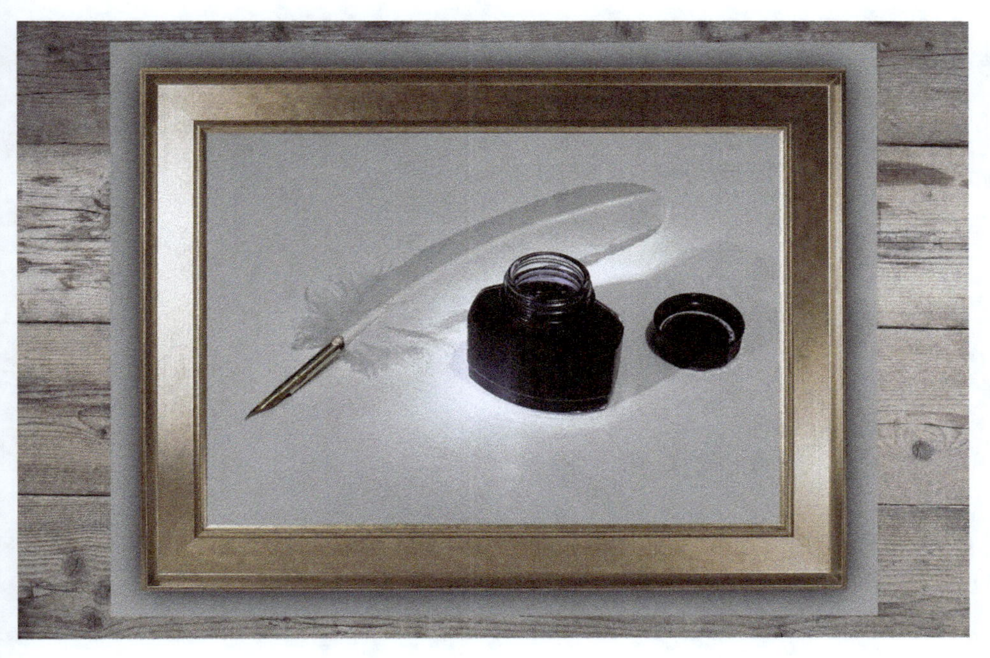

Quill and Ink

Poetry!

Poetry
Is elementary
You don't have to know a thing!

Let it flow
Then you will know
Absolutely everything!

From King Solomon
To Tweedledum
And his brother Tweedledee

Manifestations
Of versification
Have been universally aplenty!

So, take your pen
And only then
Can you make a mark

When you've begun
And when you're done
You'll be singing in your heart

Drinking gin
Whilst listening
Is what I recommend

After second shot
You'd of lost the plot
The best way to reach the end!

The Albert Einstein Limericks

Albert Einstein was a theoretical physicist
Widely acknowledged to be one of the greatest
With 300 scientific papers
He is synonymous with 'genius'
And known to influence philosophical scientists

Not the theory of general relativity
But the one of special relativity
Symbolically: $E = mc^2$
It cannot be compared
To any other in terms of memorability

The published Annus Mirabilis papers
Were the most definitive for sages
The year was 1905
Setting physics alive
Changing views on space, time and matter for ages

He discovered the photoelectric effect
Which really is just another quantum mechanic
Modern physics' second pillar
One application the semi-conductor
Einstein – an original in all things scientific

Equines

'I drift… drifting… falling into
a deep and drifting, dreamy sleep…

"'I see, yes… that's it
myself racing, yes, racing... I leap!

"'and land on a sandy beach
Madame Elite is also racing

"'Racing, racing just running and racing
We are both bareback and bare feet…'"

The waves are low and rush
They rush, not touching the horses' feet

Elizabeth Windsor

Amen, we say, God bless our serving ma'am
Seventy years since the coronate's choir sang
Steady at the helm since her reign began

Our queen has made the record book
All eyes to her this year will look
Celebrate our world-class monarch

Head of the Commonwealth lands
Sovereign of the Garter, and
Supreme Governor of the Church of England

750 holiday cards issued every year
1,500 puddings to employees far and near
Philanthropic activity beyond compare

Her first corgi was called Susan by name
A lover of horses and the equine game
And owns unmarked mute swans on the River Thames

Her Royal Highness and Majesty
Is also a lover of photography
And taking pictures of her family

To Scottish dancing she is partial
Hosting balls at Balmoral Castle
And Highland cuisine as traditional

Christmas message broadcast on the day
Telegram message on your 100th birthday
And media message honouring citizens – hooray!

Steady at the helm since her reign began
Seventy years since the coronate's choir sang
Amen, we say, God bless our serving ma'am!

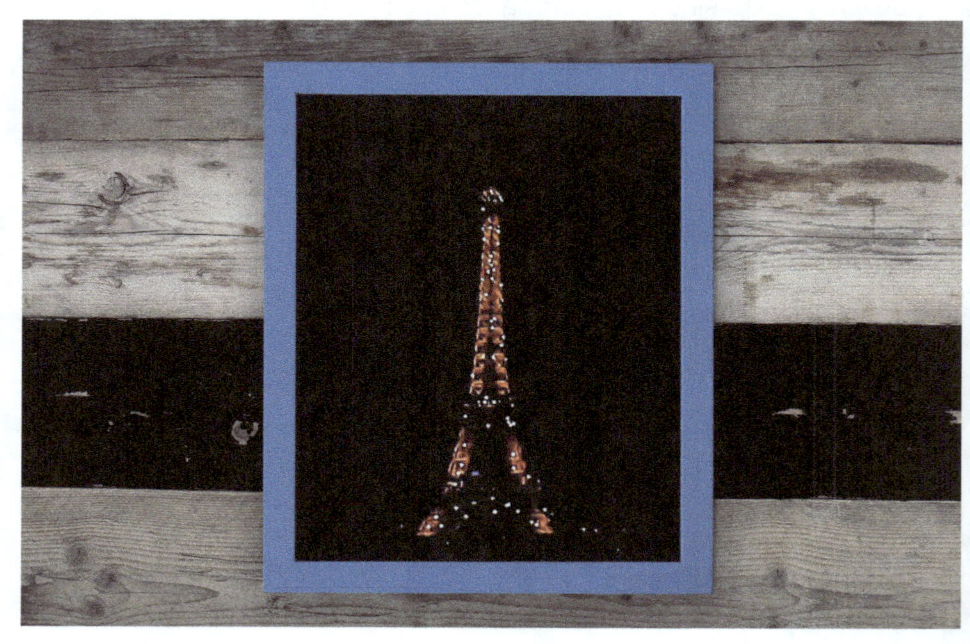

Eiffel Tower

The Twinkling Eiffel Tower

Buses here… buses there…
They jostle and jostle
Around and around
Around and around
They jostle and jostle
Buses here… buses there…

It is midnight and I sight
The twinkling Eiffel Tower's lights

Cars nudge along bit by bit
Inch by inch they move along
Stopping here… stopping there…
Stopping here… stopping there…
Inch by inch they move along
Cars nudge along bit by bit

It is midnight and I sight
Paris' iconic Christmas Tree lights

People stop… people stare…
They wander on the rue
They wonder at the Eiffel Tower

Queen Elizabeth II passes away
The Eiffel Tower's lights remain off

They wonder at the Eiffel Tower
They wander on the rue
People stop…! And stare…

So romantic at night
The twinkling Eiffel Tower's lights

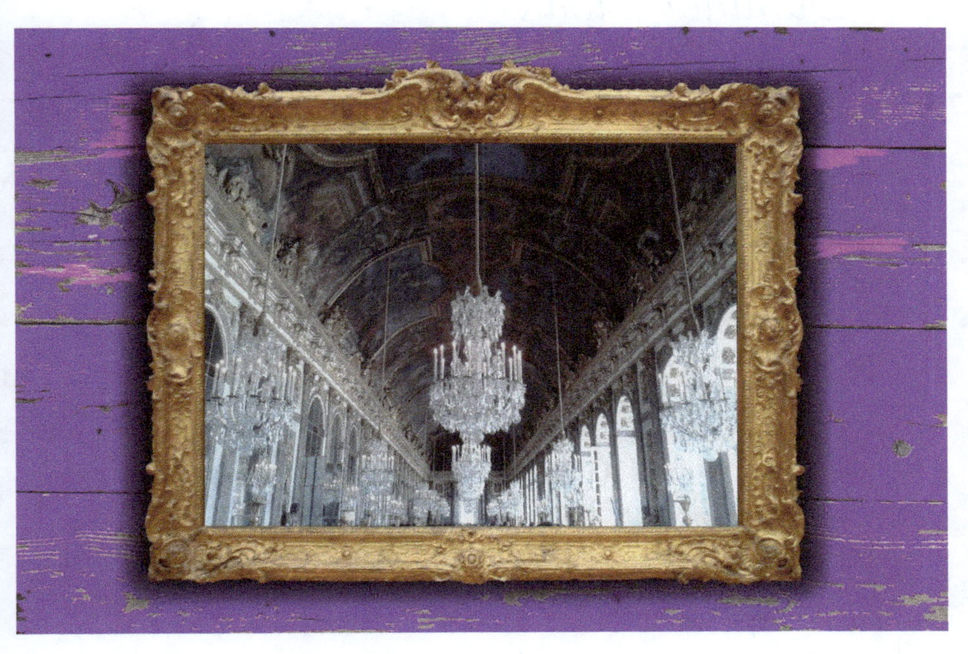

Hall of Mirrors – Versailles

Summer Clouds

Louis And Antoinette

The private, luxury jet
had just entered sky above the clouds

This sky was cobalt blue

Through the port window
Louis caught sight of a rainbow

The rainbow was no ordinary rainbow
It was dazzling and resplendent
And its shape was
like nothing ever seen on Earth
Not an arc
But a circle
A spectacular 360°!
A pure concentric
arrangement of

Red
Orange
Yellow
Green
Blue
Indigo
Violet

Sometimes you have to leave Earth
to see certain things…

"Antoinette, darling
Can you tell the pilot to change course
and fly through
the centre of that rainbow?"

"Yes, dearest"

The jet's rudder and flaps
come into operation
And as the centre of gravity alters
the Château Cheval Blanc
almost escapes the flutes

As he throttles
the pilot decides
they may like some music
to enhance the fly through

On the first strike of the
composer's staff
Louis presses a button on
the seat controls

The seats Antoinette and Louis are on
smoothly slide back
making room
for them to dance

Louis rises from his seat

Antoinette rises from her seat

They both turn to each other

Louis removes his hat and bows graciously
Plumes lightly brushing the floor

Antoinette curtsies
Tilting her head slightly forward

In time with the music
they make proud struts
Clockwise then anticlockwise

A French baroque dance ensues…

As the jet continues
a ray of sunlight strikes the flutes
bouncing light all around the inside of the aircraft

Halfway through the dance
the composer's staff
strikes a louder dynamic
And the pilot throttles to Mach 1

The g-force causes their drinks to spill – a little

They both collapse into chairs
Turn on the rearview cameras
and watch the circular rainbow
vanish into the distance
Powered by Rolls-Royce

The pilot then gently takes them back down
through the clouds and they see
the curvature of Earth again

Louis turns to Antoinette
And Antoinette turns to Louis

The pilot then announces
their estimated time of arrival…

Even though they are below
the summer clouds –
the dense, thick clouds –
bright sunlight is still bouncing around
the inside of the aircraft…!

Elements Mysterious

The sky, the sky?
I don't know why
I am so curious
Of elements mysterious

The sky, the sky
Why are you so high?
White, black, red, blue
Life on Earth pays due

The sky, the sky
Where planets pass by
Stars and black holes
Sea of emptiness unfolds

The sky, the sky
Where angels pass by
A supernatural dimension
An everywhere location

Love

To name a feeling
So deep and so strong
That lifts you to the heavens
Above the earthly throng

What is that feeling
That pumps your fleshy heart
Pumping your blood
To every organ, yes, every part?

This rich, red blood
Rich in oxygen and life
Full of nutrients and chemicals
Running red-hot emotions rife

Hormonal, irrational
Can it really be controlled?
Instinctive, emotive
The weakest of all are bold!

Your eyes
Your heart
Your mouth
Your every part!

I need you
I want you
My deepest desire
My feelings run over
My feelings on fire!

Emotions like the Sun
And all the blazing stars
No, not never
Stronger by far!

Come, your vast oceans
Do your very best
Try to quench blazing passions
Do your very best!

I call on psychology
Do try and persuade
What chemistry and biology
And physics has made

Come on, psychology
Do your very best
Try harder, try harder!
Surely, you are the best!

Bring every single theory
That you have ever conceived
To bear upon the heart
To weaken its bare knees

Much more mighty
Is love than all of this
Just a taste, a drop
And forever you are in bliss

This bliss is like a melody
Sung from the courts of heaven
Echoing the heart beats of angels
And is never forgotten

This bliss is like a melody
That has no beginning
It just was, and is
Spinning and spinning and spinning

Spinning your rich, red blood
Spinning your pumping heart
Spinning your red-hot emotions
All, all spinning – and spinning apart

Spinning your eyes
Spinning your heart
Spinning your mouth
Spinning your every part

Spinning the sun, moon
And blazing, oh, blazing stars!
Spinning the spinning oceans
That once was above the stars

Spinning the best of chemistry
In all its liquid parts
Spinning the best of biology
In all its human parts
Spinning the best of physics
In all its logical parts

And spinning
Yes, spinning
Life at its very heart

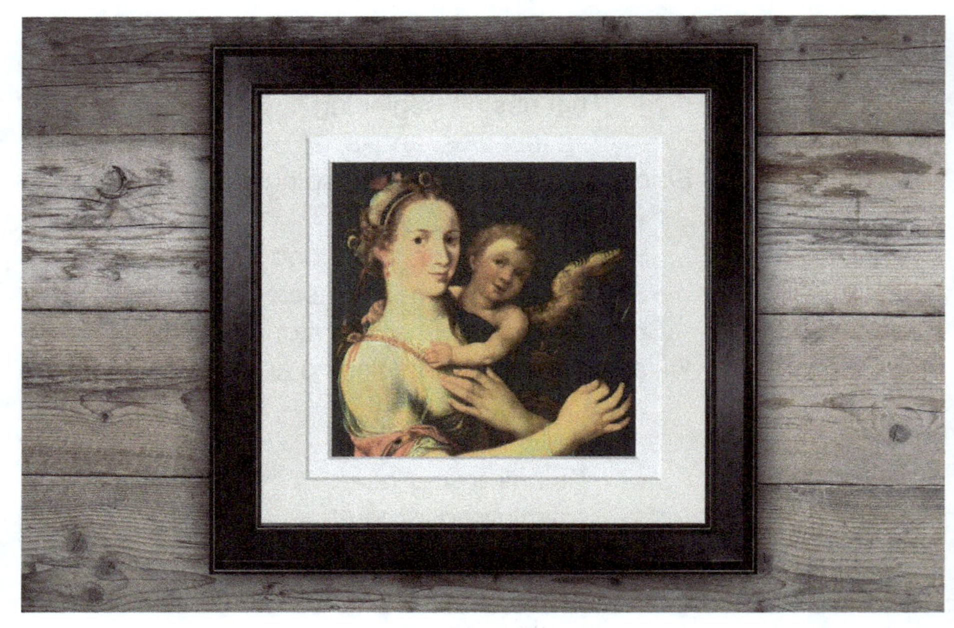

Venus and Cupid

The Finds Of Cupid

Making mortals irresistibly attractive
Cutie Cupid, heavens angel of love
With bow and arrow that never miss
His finds are unimaginably thus thereof

The bow is fashioned gold's excess
Captured from stellar supernova
The string is first Eve's lengthy tress
Twisted and spun over and over

To arrow's shaft is hardened sinews
Fallen from flailing, flying, fiery dragons
The arrow's head is forgotten truths
From the tip of the last unicorn

Making mortals irresistibly attractive
Cutie Cupid, heavens angel of love
With bow and arrow that never miss
His finds are unimaginably thus above

Madame Maclynn

Today I shared a cin cin
With the gentlewoman from Rachel Maclynn

We had breakfast at Tiffany's
Which is always a breeze

Lunch at the Opera House
Followed by Die Fledermaus

Tea on the roof of The Ritz
Then lounged about on the chintz

After dining experience at the Shard
We followed the route of the Bard

Then canapés and cocktails and caviar
At Brook Street's Claridge's Bar

What a hoot to share a cin cin
With the gentlewoman from Rachel Maclynn!

Margaret

Margaret...
Take me to the hills
Margaret...
Take me to the place
...where we are running
...as fast as fast can be

Margaret...
Take me to the place
Where I can see you

Margaret...
Take me to the wind
Margaret...
Take me to the place
...where we are flying
...as high as high can be

Margaret...
Take me to the place
Where I can see you

I'm run... ning!

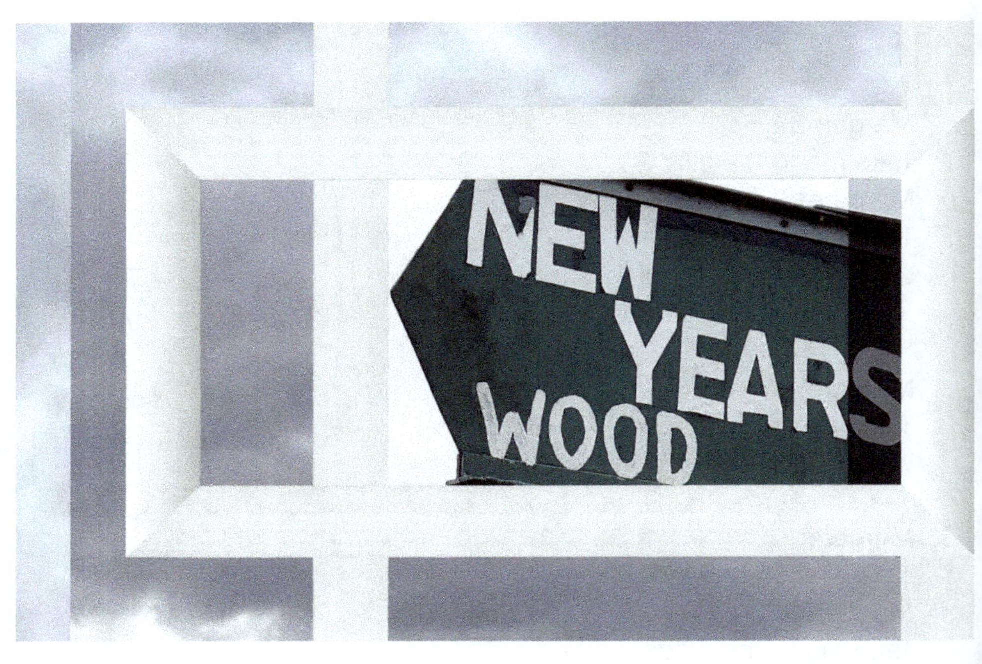

New Years Wood

Oranges And Tangerines

Oranges and tangerines
Satsumas and clementines
2022 is fresh and clean
Happy New Year, sweet Caroline!

Thoughts of the future
Come around this time
New Year music and culture
Growing rosemary and thyme

Riding a tandem bicycle
Drinking vintage red wine
Such are the thoughts of Michael
What are yours, sweet Caroline?

Even though it's January
The weather is quite fine
Mild and dry and sunny
And birdsong in the garden of mine

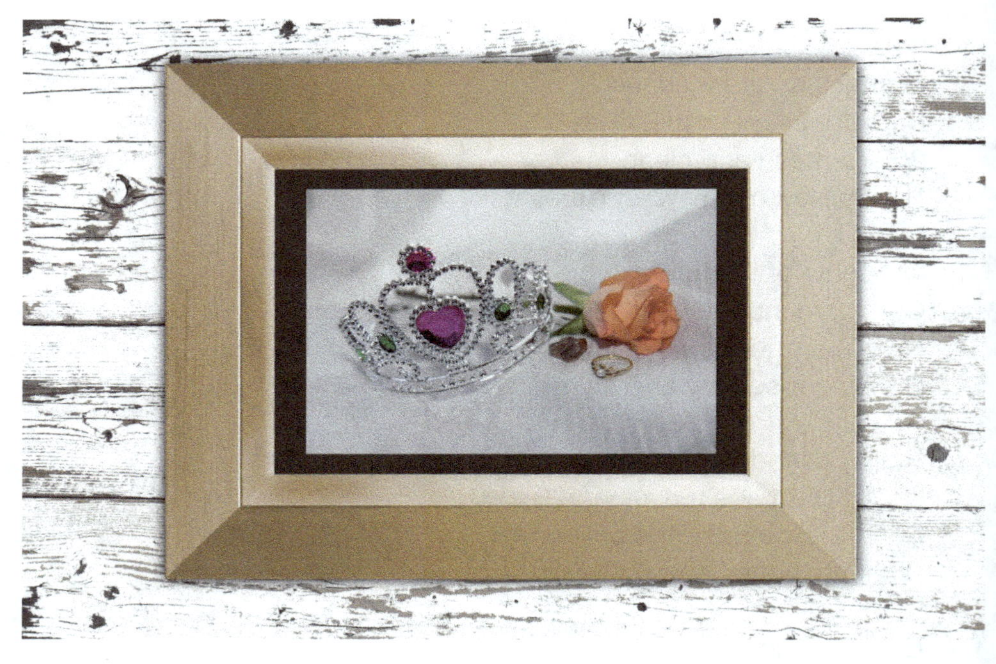

The Wedding

"I Want To Get Married!"

"I want to get married!" Chris Martin cried
"And hear the pitter-patter of two tiny feet
Living with my little babe and beautiful bride
And fulfilment at work, what could be more complete?"

That's what he hoped and dreamed a year or more ago
But he tried too hard for his efforts were no good
So he took up many pursuits adding strings to his bow
Crashing and fixing cars, exercise and fast food

But during last summer living it up in Spain
Playing on the beach and getting sand in his hair
Chris met Lisa and saw fit to contain
The friendship that followed and enjoyed by the pair

"Would this be just another holiday romance?"
They both painfully thought when it was time to leave
"Or the introduction to something with substance
Turning into a kinship we both could believe?"

As time came to pass the latter thought became true
And fervent feelings flowed between these turtle doves
Gifts and candlelight dinners keeps their love strong and new
Will it last a lifetime? Who knows but God above

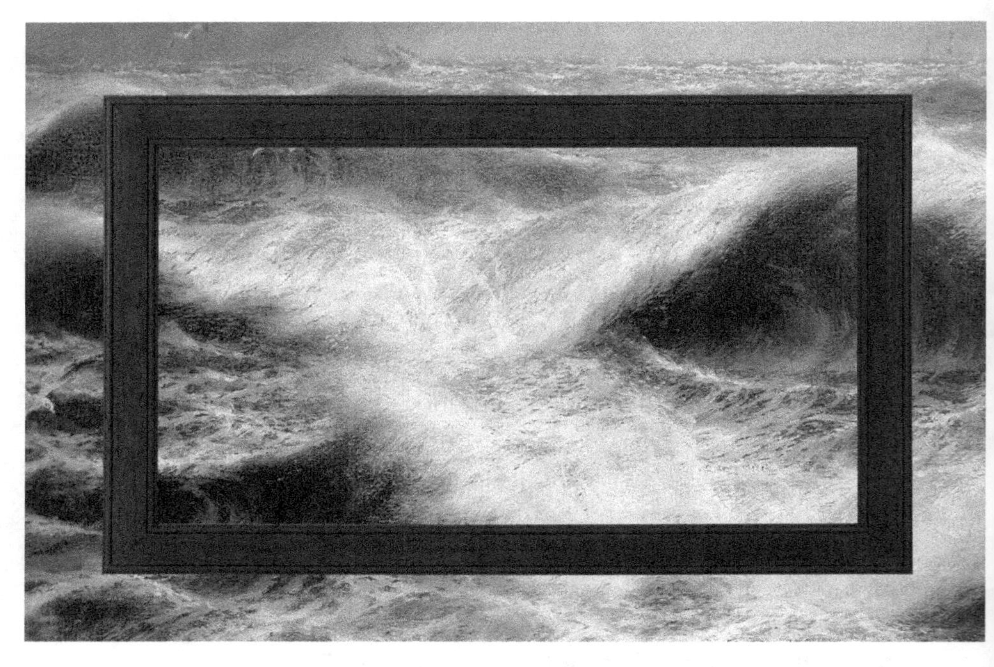

In Caernarvon Bay

The Incredible, Credible Sea

At The Mariner's Inn I did meet
The incredible, credible Marguerite
Her seafaring credentials were complete

She decided to journey me – the yacht
Crossing the tees and dotting the dots
And sealing the deal with a sheepshank knot

Myself as coxswain at the helm
We set out on the watery realm
Not allowing the elements to overwhelm

Genoa sailing ropes firmly in the hand
Reaching energy filled man and man
Streaking away the catamaran!

With The Wash to the lee
And behind the North Sea
We rounded the coast East An'gli

The mainsail's battens eager to streak
Ahead of the wind in a dancing gigue
Ahead of the stretching, stretching league

Just into the English Channel
The elements began to funnel
To all our boat – oh, the pummel!

Despite the keen, gale force wind
Our course maintained without rescind
Hopping the chopping waves and wind

Setting again and again for Thatches
But stronger Beaufort hurriedly dispatches
And genoa ropes slips and snatches

…an albatross scurries the bows…
So, we tack and head for Cowes!

The wind whips with wanton water
Wrests all sunlight to low – to falter
Point-blank vision the dreaded order

For fear the dreaded, dreaded capsize
We lower the mainsail and foresail by size
An S.O.S. mingles with the wretched skies

The incredible, credible Marguerite
Perform's incredibly, credible feats
She takes soundings and then repeats

Descending: fifty… forty… then twenty-one
And that's when our prayers reached a ton
And that's when our prayers reached a ton

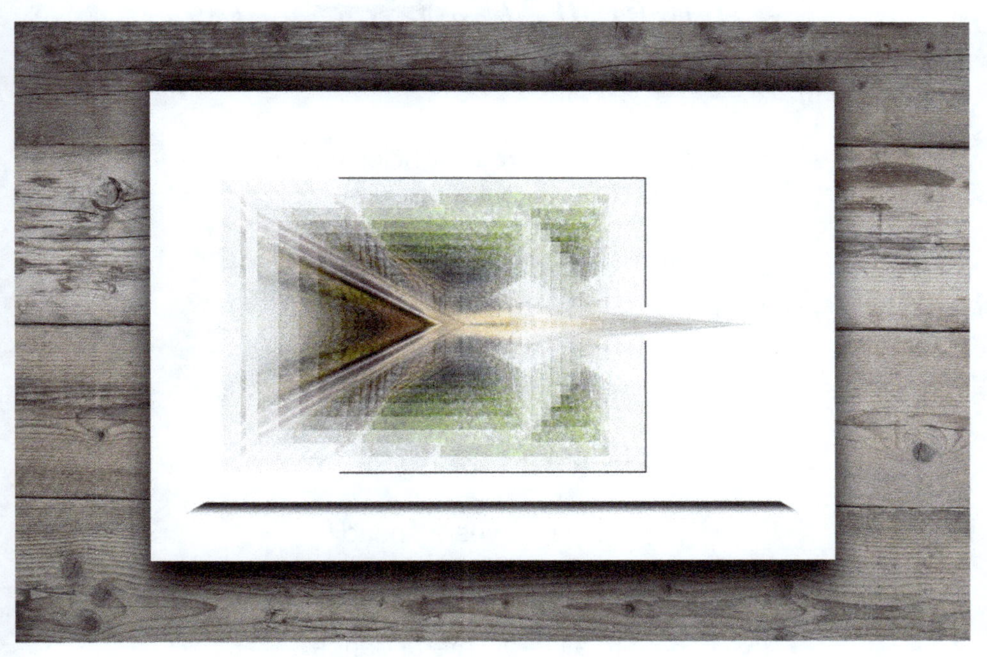

Saint Conan's Arrow

https://www.ne-plus-ultra.co.uk

Michael Angelo Bobb
Artist Of The ~~Past~~ Future

* "A real highflier
Mixing with the elite"
Cries the town crier
"Extraordinary artistic feats!"

* 'Get high on me
Drink my creative juice
Eat from my tree
Forget the golden goose'

* Light years ahead
Science has no chance
The future he has led
In a literal, lateral dance

* Out of this world
His art is fantastic!
An abstract cosmic twirl
Interplanetary, intergalactic

* Tripping the light fantastic
Warping space and time
Quantum realms elastic
Pristine art, pristine enzymes

* Ne Plus Ultra
Apotheosis art
Entirely of culture
Two-part art

* Ne Plus Ultra
Wonders to impart
Entirely of culture
Art in two parts

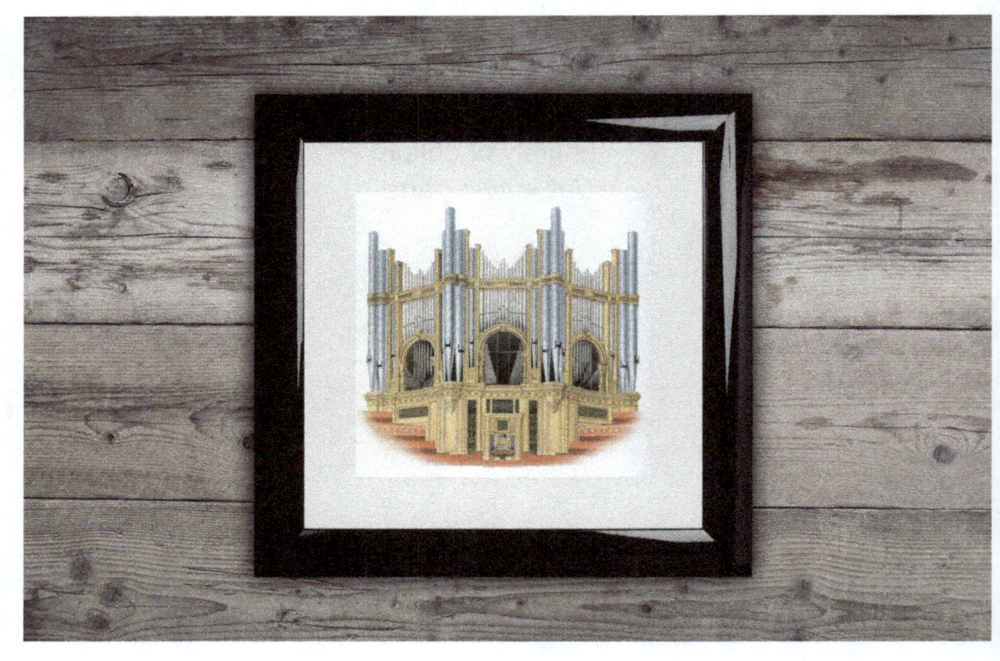

Organ

Toccata In D Minor

The most famous piece of organ music ever written
From the very first notes it demands your attention
Bombastic, outlandish and downright ostentatious
Sweeping and catchy proverbs flowing continuous

Could J. S. Bach have written it before breakfast
A mere virtuosic piece in the style of a tempest?
It demands velocity, dexterity and an artistic touch
Aplomb musicality, measured ferocity and such

Descending into the sonorous depths of D minor
Obeying the rules of the unrequited rubato timer
Clarion dynamics arrest wavelengths sonic
This articulate toccata story is exceedingly dramatic

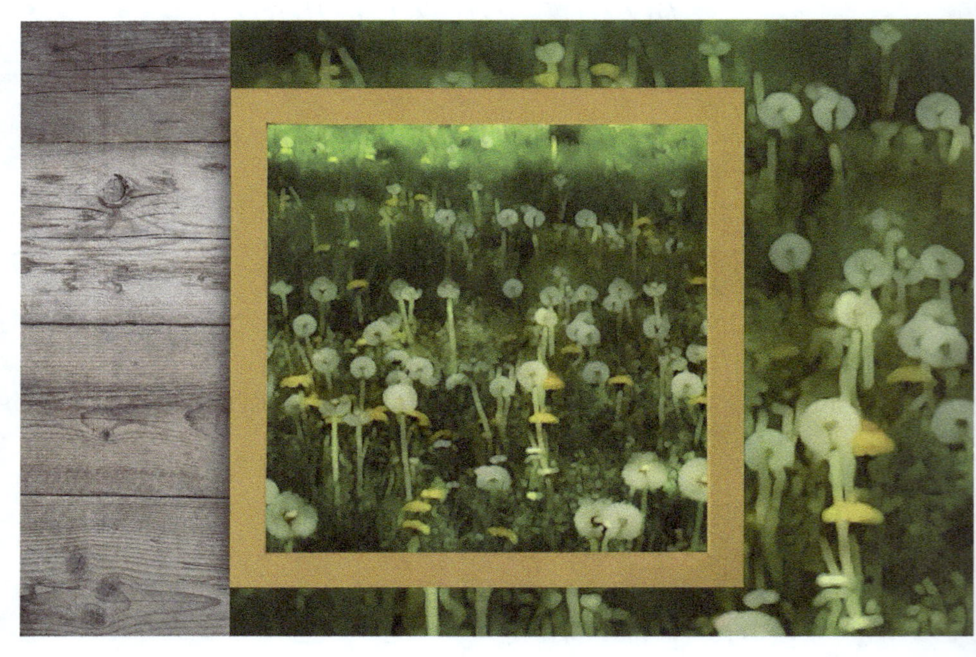

Meadow

The Bees... The Flowers... The Breeze...

A Poet's Agony

In a midafternoon, Midshire meadow
North of a cool May day
I rolled with the wind that did blow
And played with the straw and the hay

Beaming, beaming on Midshire meadow
The sun had come with fun
The moon in the sky in shadow
Sky and sun made meadow undone

Above all creatures in Midshire meadow
The honeybees were, well, just honeybees
Hopping and buzzing sweet and low
Then back to the hives on the trees

...Early the next morning
My eyes barely opening
I was thinking about the scene
My thoughts became strong
And I continued along
Thinking on what I had seen...

The bees… the flowers… the breeze…
Over and over and over
The bees… the flowers… the breeze…

I fell on fixation
Landing on obsession
Thoughts reigned again and again
In complete capitulation
I gave way to compulsion
And I stole away my pen

Around the pen the words coiled
Wrought from the depths of somewhere
For a good long while I toiled
Trying words here, there and elsewhere

…Two hours later the clock announced – bold!
"Stop, my friend, for you have struck gold
For you have written the last word
Besides, the pen has become furred!"

And only then, after returning pen
Could I live a normal life
Free from obsession, free from compulsion
Free from malady and strife

…Time for breakfast …time to continue with my day

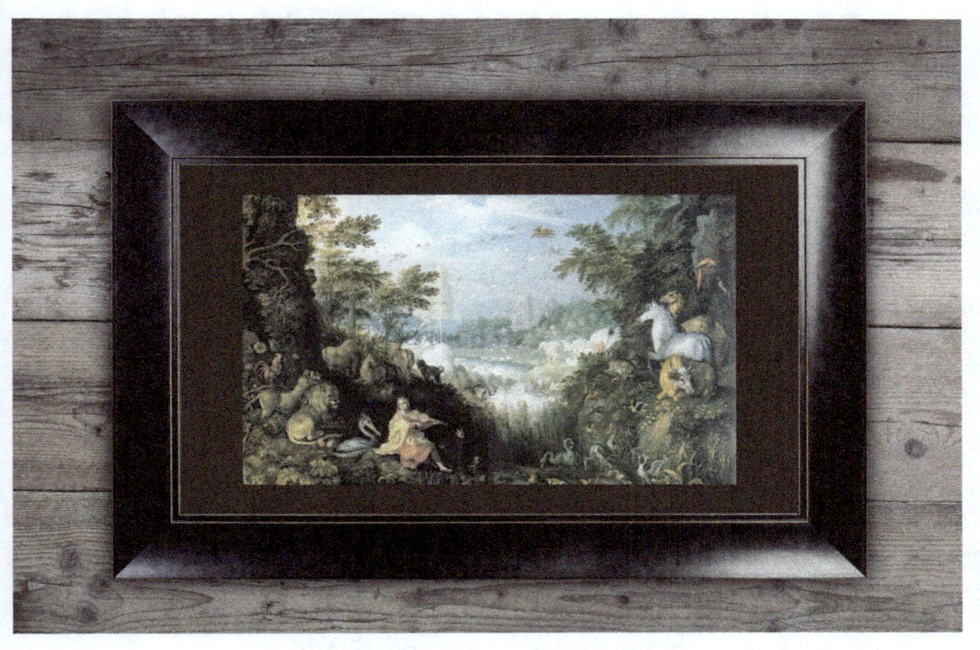

Orpheus

It's An Onomatopoeic Jungle Out There!

If a bark does poodle and bulldog
Then a hark the avian angels try
And a moo milks poor brown cow
Like a boo frightening Count Vampire

If a roar owns all lions and pussycats
Then a boar gets fed up very easily
And a hiss slides off the back of snakes
Like a kiss from a gorilla with a hanky

If a quack goes to a registrar — no, consultant
Then a duck eats doctor on toast for medicine
And a neigh is something horses roll in
Like a hay and a ho and a noddy, noddy sedition!

Mr Spock Perms Doctor Who's Hair

After cleaning the Starship's windscreen
And finishing his novel called: Illogical
Mr Spock pauses the washing machine
To wash his hair with detergent biological

As he finishes with a blow dry
In a typical Vulcan style
He decides to teleport onto the Tardis
To see Doctor Who for a while

Whilst inside the redesigned Tardis
Doctor Who moans about the Daleks
"All they ever seem to do is shout: 'Exterminate!'
I'm fed up with it all – sick!"

"What you need, Doctor, is a new hairstyle
It also doubles as a weapon
When the Daleks see your perm," Spock says
"Their alien brains will go into meltdown"

Mr Spock begins and proceeds
To wind locks of hair around each finger
Using Vulcan breath as hairspray
And occasional licks to add moisture

After a good ninety-five minutes
According to Earth's time zone
Doctor Who has a full set of curls
And is ready to take on the arch-foe

Suddenly, the enemy attack is sounded
So Doctor Who checks his hair in the mirror
And heads straight for the front line
To make the Daleks shake like never

As soon as the Daleks see his perm
Their brains overheat and melt down
Turning, they attack each other
Tip over and fall to the ground

No longer will they shout: "Exterminate!"
In that screeching, terrifying voice
At the end of a cliffhanging episode
Causing you to hide with your toys

Mr Spock returns to the Starship
Perming the entire crew at warp speed
This newfound hairstyle weapon
Will make the Klingons weak as weeds

Just another day on the Starship Second Prize
Tomorrow's episode promises more
As they continue on their Great Commission:
"To boldly go where no Time Lord has gone before!"

Burn After Reading!

"Your assignment
if you choose to accept
is to write about fishing

"Anything else
would be in contempt
except for dishwashing!"

That was the directive
from the Secret Service
a.k.a. the Croydon Poetry Hour

So here is the poem
written with absurdness
to while away the hour

The idea what to write
came during another sport
the sport of intensive ironing

So, pressing creases
or anything of the sort
produces great imagining!

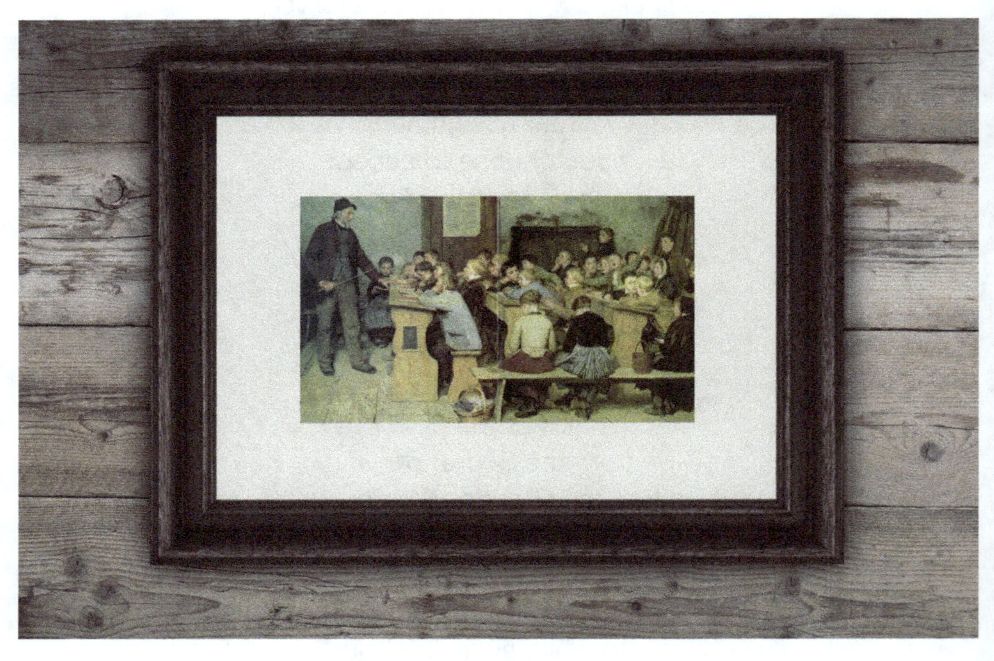

Archiv fur Kunst und Geschichte

What NOT To Say When You Have Been Invited To Speak At A School Assembly

"Thank you for inviting me
to the school assembly
I really feel quite honoured.
Students these days
need not follow the craze
of trying to achieve high grades
so don't even bother!

"I am an example
of watching Miss Marple
at least two times a week.
Rubbish in drama tuition
but great in stealing gold bullion
and the illegal trade of ammunition
plus, how to make false antiques.

"My best ever lesson
was during a science session
when the teacher made a mistake.
Pouring masses and masses
of paraffin on live electrical apparatus
just to see what gases
would escape.

"However, it wasn't all bad
when I was a lad
I wasn't quite 'the nutter'.
You see,
I was a hit with the girls
preferring brunettes with curls
especially daughters of Earls
and giving them rides on my scooter.

"And now I have got
a catamaran yacht
regularly sailing the high seas.
A twenty-bed mansion
and a £100K pension
— no time for taking lessons —
and do whatever I please!"

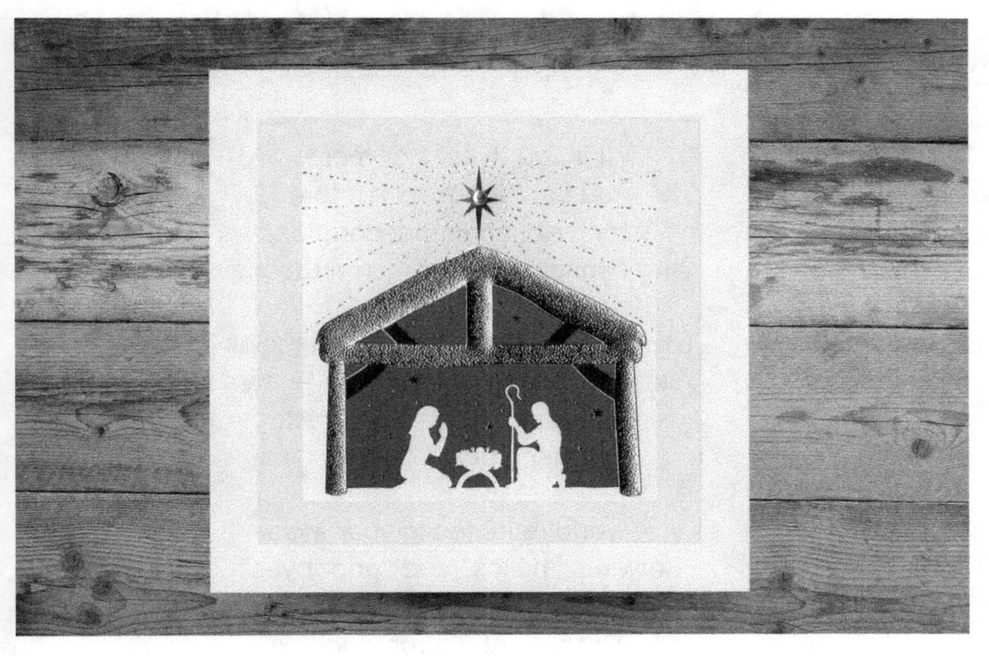

The Nativity

Advantageous Advent

It is four weeks or more
And I am at the local store
Gazing at hanging decorations
And I imagine choral murmurations

There is a kind of busyness in the air
Yes, an increase in busyness — care
Exchanged and expressed
Just a hint, I guess

A world reflected in your eyes
Between "hullos" and "goodbyes"
Not just in the stores
But also at church doors

There is hope for a Saviour
That will end man's hard labour
He was, and is, a King
And peace and joy He will bring

Advent calendar will soon be here
With chocolate and pictures of those dear
Some calendars will have behind each door
A burst of Christmas colours galore

These preparations help us to prepare
For the season's festival and fares
As for me, I tap wrapping paper on the pass
And wish the checkout lady, "Happy Christmas"

The Eve Of The Great Eve

Today is the 23rd of December
and all the parties
will soon come to an end
Shops will be starting to close
and the minds of men
will be given to Christmas

Offices and pubs and transport
will follow the minds
of all Christmas men
All these in humble preparation
All will be closed tomorrow
before the last o'clock p.m.

Tomorrow is the Great Eve
No calendar date is as great as this eve
But, we will have to wait
I so dearly hope that
this Great Eve will not be late

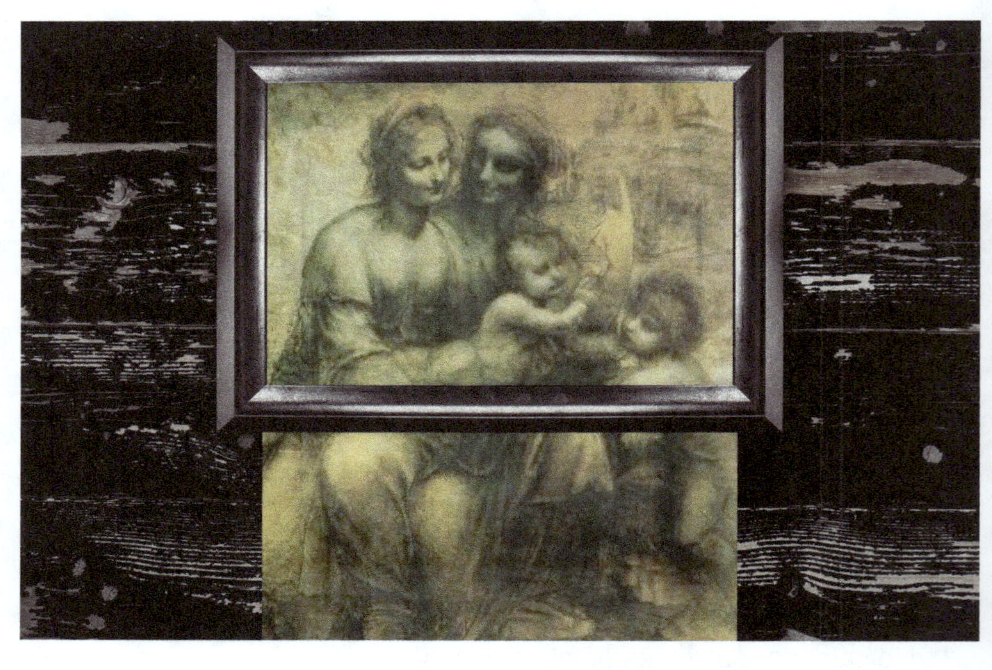

La Vie à l'enfant avec sainte Anne
et saint Jean-Baptiste

Christmas Greetings One And All!

Andrew

It's celebration time
For all and Andrew
God becoming flesh
Too true, too true

Angela

Such a delight
With truth and light
Posts spun: this Advent Calendar
She captured the occasion
With seasoned celebration
Did she, the writer, Angela!

Eleanor

Season's greetings
For neighbour Eleanor
Hoping that 2022
Will be even better

Ian

It's Christmastime
Enjoy it Ian
Best wishes to your family
And every human being

Joe

Merry Christmas
Big Issue, Joe
Happy New Year, too
Whatever your
Hopes and dreams
May they all come true

Julie

The angel did sing
Today, born an offering
Celebrate Judeo-Christian, Julie!
Saving the human soul
And washing feet with a bowl
Ascribe to Him God's great glory

Nemone

Season's greetings
To dearest Nemone
Enjoy the mistletoe
Enjoy the holly

Pam

Happy Christmas
To Cumbrian Pam
Celebrating Jesus
The Son of the I AM

Patrick and Yvonne

Tis the season to be jolly
Patrick and Yvonne Webster
Hope you both make time
For drinks and much laughter

Peter and Judi

In complete fulfilment
God's son was sent
To deliver Peter and Judi
Since history's ages
Sought by sages
Such was said verily, verily

Processing Center

It's Christmastime, it's Christmastime!
Enjoy Processing Center
Jesus is the true reason
Come in 2022, do enter

Ron and Sheila

Warm wishes this season
Celebrating the reason
Happy Christmas Ron and Sheila
Jesus Christ came to earth
In a truly miraculous birth
My Lord, my God, my Saviour!

SE20 Art Group

Happy Christmas everyone!
Celebrate God's Son!
Artists SE and 20
Let's tread the New Year
Boldly and with flair
Artworks varied and plenty!

Shanthi

Season's greetings
To dearest Shanthi
Baubles and tinsel
On Christmas tree

It's time for celebrations
Tidings of great joy
Jesus Begotten
Emmanuel, the Boy

Terry

Tidings of great joy
For jolly Terry
Hoping the season
Is making you merry

Trevor and Julie

It's Christmastime!
It's Christmastime!
Our Saviour came not early
Prophesied
Then He died
For Trevor and for Julie

Sleigh Ride

Swaying… sleighing…
Moving this way
Then that way

Swerving… sliding…
Then another way
Then that way

Such a joy to ride
Santa by my side

Down the mountainside
Dodging trees of pine

Sleeting… snowing…
Such a joy to ride
Santa by my side

Beaming… laughing…
Down the mountain side
Dodging trees of pine

Swaying… sleighing…
Moving this way
Then that way

Swerving… sliding…
Then another way
Then that way

Such a joy to ride
Santa by my side

Down the mountainside
Dodging trees of pine

Sleeting… snowing…
Such a joy to ride
Santa by my side

Beaming… laughing…
Down the mountainside
Dodging trees of pine

Beaming… laughing…
Down the mountain-
side
    side
        side
            side
                side
                    side

Dodging trees of
Pine
    pine
        pine
            pine
                pine
                    pine

Down the mountainSIDE!

Come, Emmanuel, Meet Us

Many happy returns
Of the season, Jesus
May You find faith on Earth

Turning, turning the year turns
Come, Emmanuel, meet us

May You find faith on Earth
Sweet, Darling Jesus
Born a babe to save mankind

Turning, turning the year turns
Come, Emmanuel, meet us

Many are the woes of man
Agape You gave, Jesus
Repent and turn to Him

Turning, turning the year turns
Come, Emmanuel, meet us

Come, let us all agree
The year of the Lord is Jesus
A.D. 2022 has almost gone

Turning, turning the year turns
Come, Emmanuel, meet us

What will the New Year bring
Come, Emmanuel, meet us
God alone holds the keys
Come, Emmanuel, meet us
Come, Emmanuel, meet us!

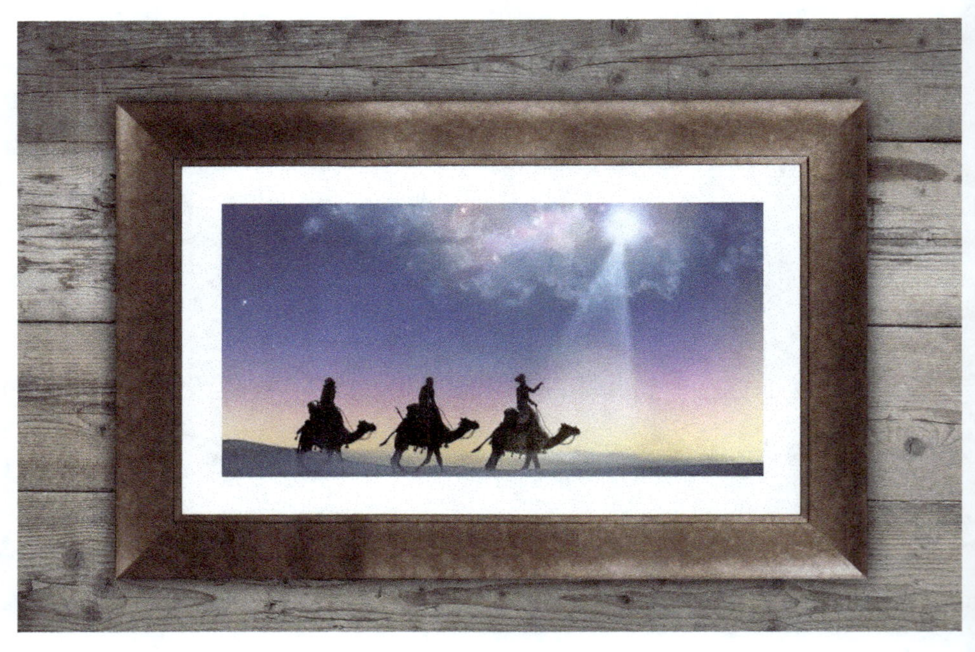

Three Wise Men

The Alternative Three Wise Men

From all the way in Lapland
To Bethlehem to make an entry
Hurried Father Christmas and Rudolf
Wearing their green panties

Father Christmas gave a pair of lace-up boots
That were bigger than any stocking size
He also gave a shaving kit
To be used after Jesus was baptised

Mr Spock beamed down from the Starship Enterprise
His journey started on the other side of the Galaxy
His gift for the very young babe
Was a tube of coloured Smarties

He also had other gifts
From planets far and wide
But he lost them all
When the Enterprise fell on its side

The third wise man everybody knows
He composed music for the Tsars in Russia
He is tall and really quite lanky
I know him as Sergei Rachmaninoff

His gift wasn't really special
And has to be played with the left toe
Softly and quietly – a lullaby for a King –
A full-size grand piano

Today Is Twelfth Night!

Today is Twelfth Night
Or What You Will
Scribbles, Billy Shakespeare
With ink and feathered quill

He writes in comedic fashion
Love thrown in and weaves the right
Serious fool Malvolio grins
With cross-gartered yellow tights

But before all the shenanigans
The Bard scribbles ever anon
The famous line from all the play
"If music be the food of love
dear boy, please, do play on"

Torn!

In times BC
God's people couldn't see
The glory and wonder of the LORD

A curtain in place
We couldn't see His face
Only priests dare went to the LORD

In fear we stayed
Our seeing kept, veiled
Could not go direct to the Father

But now the veil is gone
Torn from top to bottom
And Jesus bids us, "Enter!"

The sufficient cross
Removed more than dross
But now we, too, are loved sons

Running straight in
Free from all our sin
Face to face, unveiled — His loved ones!

God Has Decided

Lockdowns, lockdowns
All around
How many towns?
Shutdown, shutdown
All around!

Isolation
Contemplation
What does it mean?
Sickness?
Sickness!
Quarantine!

Have you ever seen
Such an epic scene…!

Catching all the world
In an epic twirl…!

Solitary seclusion
Absolute isolation

Just you by yourself
And no one else!

Not a manly touch
Nor a female touch
But God is much
With a godly touch!

In all the nunneries
In all the monasteries
Shout, honey eating prophet…!
Forty days in the wilderness
Fasting the baptised Jesus
Diabolos defeated – deficit!

And all the Saints
That never faint
From time immemorial…
On bended knee
And fasting glee
Engage the supernatural…

All alone
And by yourself
Abject and pathetic…
Life a loan
From God Himself
Other gods pathetic…

Enforced lockdowns
Please, do not frown
Or be in denial…
God had decided
Yes, even commanded
A secret revival!

All in a flash
Yes, twenty minutes
Secret did waft…
A concluding tune
Entered my mind
Bach's 'Wachet Auf'

Tongues

Forecasts, forecasts
Satellite predictions?
Meteorological predictions?
God's directions!
 Storm, lightning, thunder!

Preaching, preaching
Pastor teaching
Christians hearing
Everyone wanting
 Storm, lightning, thunder!

Spiritual gifting
Very uplifting
Be receiving
Hands imparting
 Storm, lightning, thunder!

Myself overhearing
Two conversing
Spirit interrupting
Myself imparting
 Storm, lightning, thunder!

…weather calm
No alarm
Hours pass
Not for long
No storm, no lightning, no thunder

Climbing hill
Clouds roll in
Chiaroscuro
Darker still
Storm? Lightning? Thunder?

Up the hill
Storm rolls in
Frightening thunder!
Frightening still!

Cracking thunder!
I maintain
Lightning cracking!
I maintain
Stormy downpour!
I maintain
Up the hill
I maintain!

Oh, holy hill…!

Battle and battle
On and on
Up and up
On and on

Three quarters up
Saturated, soaked
Will I atop?
Inside I'm stoked

…Alas
Before the top
Aside I turn
Before the top

God has won
He always does
Down I come
Saturated
Head to toe

Pass the bridge
See a shop
Cello in window
I stare and stop

I hear no thunder
See no light
Feel no water
Cello fills sight…!

How long did I stay?
How long is a night…?

Forecasts, forecasts
Satellite predictions?
Meteorological predictions?
God's directions!
Storm, lightning, thunder!
The heavens rent asunder!

. . .

"Remove your shoes
for the hill you are on
is holy"

Here The Deities Approve

**In the first year of
Charles III
King of the United Kingdom**

A Monday…
The Monday
Monday 24th October
Midnight plus an hour and a half
or thereabouts

A message comes through
on my iPad Pro…
On the surface
an ordinary message
To a trained life
this is not ordinary!

Alert
Intrigued
Compelled

Russia
Russia
It's from Russia

An EARLYMUSIC subscription
notifying me of their new post…
The composer is Henry Purcell
YouTube the platform host…

Michael Chance the countertenor
Nigel North's lute improve
The photo: St.-Petersburg
The music: 'Here The Deities Approve'

My spirit in strong discernment
My soul compelled to action
My mind uneasy and unsettled
My heart in mysterious contemplation…

Myself the nerd
checks the time
of the posting…
My view third
A multi-paradigm!
In God I'm boasting!

Compelled, compelled I must share
Compelled again, must share – must share!

And so I do
In that hours
One site rings true
Site's music thread towers

Compelled again
I make a note
Compelled, compelled
Calendar smote

Rational, emotional
or Holy Spiritual…?
Ask all the gods
if this was God!

———

…After some sleep I rise
and continue with my day

iPad Pro lights up again
Apple News notification…
Rishi Sunak is the next Prime Minister
over the British Nation…
The Conservative Party
voted him in
the day before
before evening hymn…

iPad Pro refreshes again
This time it's an
email notification…
From the same site I posted to
a few hours earlier
An incredible, credible affirmation…

It's the same thread
but someone else has posted
another piece of music
and coincidences beg to be roasted
– alive!

It's an OTD post:
The Composer: Benjamin Britten
The music: 'Voices for Today'
Premiered 24th October 1965

Of all the pieces written!

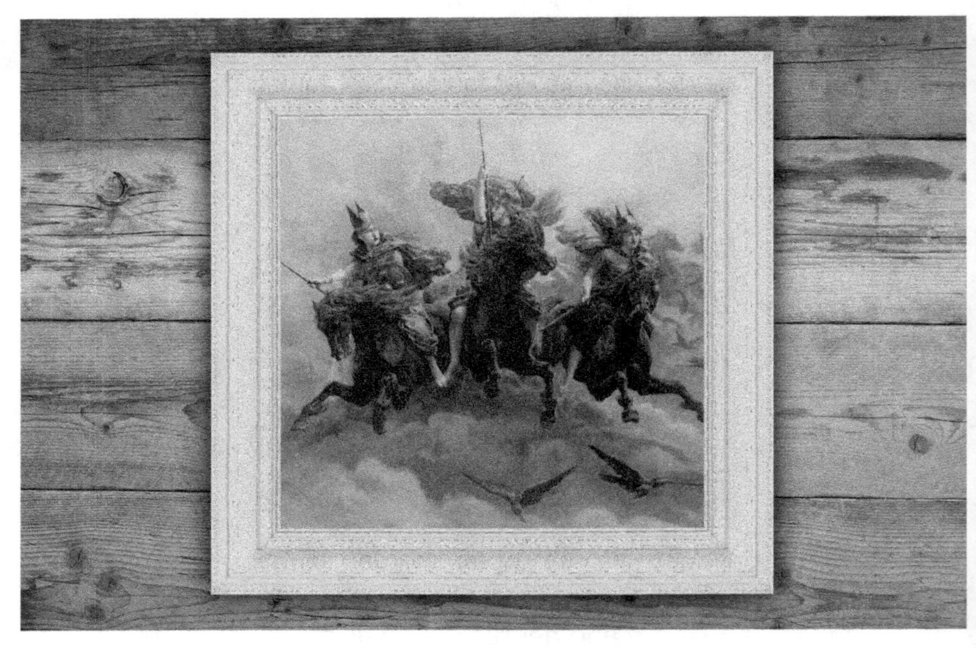

Valkyries

Alberich

On his journeyed life he had reached the point
To put to an end every suffering exploit
At the hands of ill, heathen men
For their toxic deeds were 10 out of 10

Came this winter after autumn's fall
That very apex, the summit of all
Almighty God's clockwork wise
Forcing all ungodly into demise
God Almighty, his soul He caught
And timely, conscious early thought

The timely, conscious thought was in
Destroy every document of sin
The timely soundtrack came in too
Almighty God's perfect timing – true

Wagner's Ring: 'Twilight of the gods'
Concluded the day against all odds
This final act of the great opera, an epic
Timed the same time as thoughts of ethic

Prepared and done the scene was set
The Sword of the Spirit – any better yet!?
Red light and white light shining the scene
Binoculars ready, as ready as keen

And so to the final item – all power invested
Tried and tried and tried; tested and tested and tested
A gold ring – just one will do
He had not one… but two!

Wagner's Ring: 'Twilight of the gods'
The epic opera concludes – glory to God!
Greater glory to Him and His timely Spirit
Imparting conscious thought; an efficacious visit
To rid the world of toxic remnants
Dastardly, dangerous, deceiving documents!

Red light fiery: blazing sun
White light shining: God's glorious Son!
Bellowing airways: 'Twilight of the gods!'
The heavens convene; God giving the nods

On each sinful document he scratches, 'Alberich'
In bright, bloody red without a single blink
Tears once in half and consigns to hell
The sweet song sings and all is well...

An hour had passed – yes, even more
Since first wretched document he much tore
One by one, no, not needing to count
He piled high on high on hades mount

He took binoculars, stood back, assured
And gazed at the Spirit – the Holy Sword
Then stepped forward to finish the rout
Until all sin destroyed – yes, thrown out

On his journeyed life he had reached the stage
Where he had finally divested all that baggage
Forgiving ills of all heathen men
Forgiven! Forgiven! Forgiven!

Wagner's Ring: 'Twilight of the gods'
The gods de-create in front of God
Themselves and their realms they incinerate
Till zero is left of their pseudo state
        Then, a gold ring is placed on a finger
        As the day forgets to linger

Audiobook on Double CD

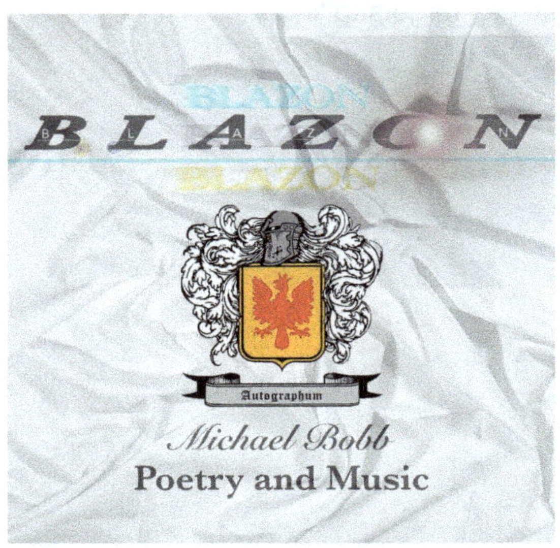

Double CD

BLAZON

CD 1 *73 min*

1	The Blazon And The Sword	3:19
2	Poetry!	2:26
3	The Albert Einstein Limericks	4:20
4	Equines	3:09
5	Elizabeth Windsor	5:14
6	The Twinkling Eiffel Tower	5:14
7	Summer Clouds	6:14
8	Elements Mysterious	6:59
9	Love	7:15
10	The Finds of Cupid	3:12
11	Madame Maclynn	3:01
12	Margaret	4:05
13	Oranges and Tangerines	2:43
14	"I Want to Get Married!"	4:35
15	The Incredible, Credible Sea	4:41
16	Michael Angelo Bobb	3:12
17	Toccata In D Minor	3:27

CD 2 *78 min*

1	The Bees... The Flowers... The Breeze...	9:11
2	It's an Onomatopoeic Jungle Out There!	2:36
3	Mr Spock Perms Doctor Who's Hair	4:51
4	Burn After Reading!	2:48
5	What NOT To Say When You Have Been Invited To Speak At A School Assembly	3:37
6	Advantageous Advent	3:25
7	The Eve Of The Great Eve	2:45
8	Christmas Greetings One And All!	7:42
9	Sleigh Ride	3:40
10	Come, Emmanuel, Meet Us	3:34
11	The Alternative Three Wise Men	3:04
12	Today Is Twelfth Night!	2:22
13	Torn!	3:42
14	God Has Decided	4:43
15	Tongues	6:37
16	Here The Deities Approve	5:52
17	Alberich	7:21

All poems written and performed by Michael Bobb

£15

AD 2023   www.theautographscore.co.uk

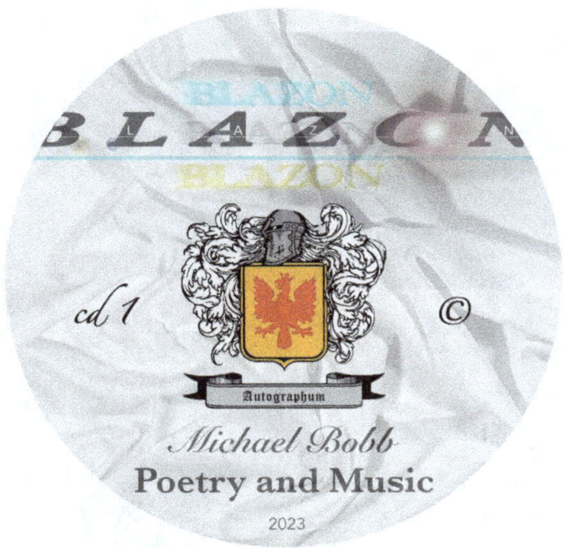
BLAZON
cd 1
Autographum
Michael Bobb
Poetry and Music
2023

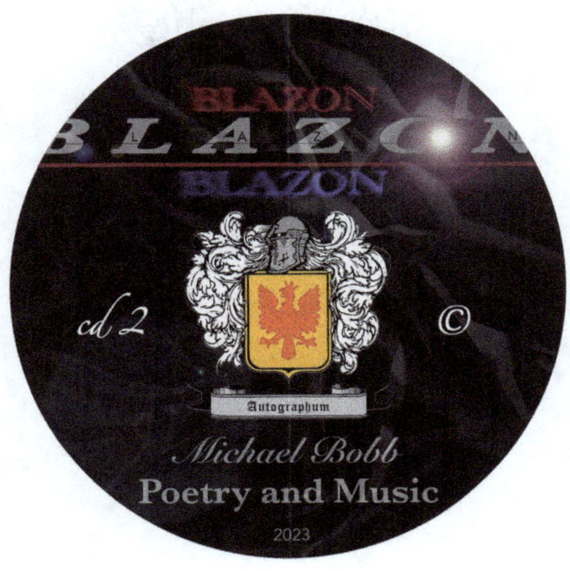
BLAZON
cd 2
Autographum
Michael Bobb
Poetry and Music
2023

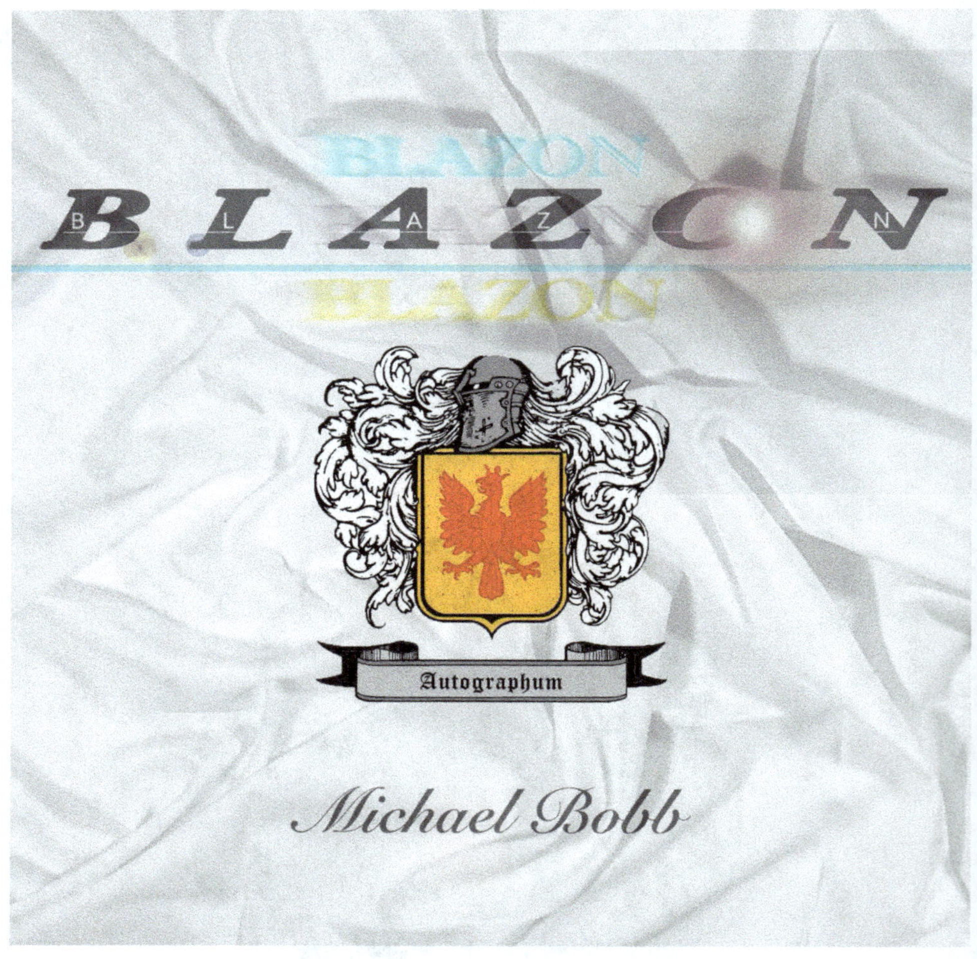
BLAZON
Autographum
Michael Bobb

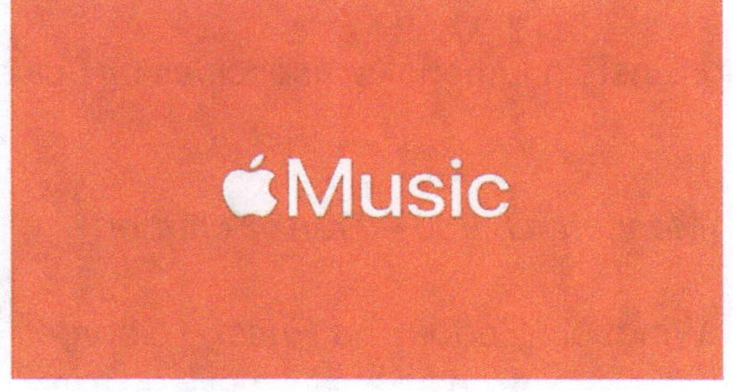

Music in Audiobook

1. The Blazon And The Sword *(Come Again – John Dowland)*

2. Poetry! *(A Little Joke – Dmitri Kabalevsky)*

3. The Albert Einstein Limericks *(Isosceles or Scalene – Michael Bobb)*

4. Equines *(Menuett, D. 600 – Franz Schubert)*

5. Elizabeth Windsor *(Zadok The Priest – George Frideric Handel)*

6. The Twinkling Eiffel Tower *(Jerusalem – Hubert Parry)*

7. Summer Clouds *(Marche Pour La Ceremomie Des Turcs – Jean-Baptiste Lully)*

8. Elements Mysterious *(Ballade Strada – Michael Bobb)*

9. Love *(Domine Deus – Antonio Vivaldi)*

10. The Finds of Cupid *(Stars and Butterflies – Dario Marianelli)*

11. Madame Maclynn *(Die Fledermaus (Overture) – Johann Strauss II)*

12. Margaret *(Margaret – Michael Bobb)*

13. Oranges and Tangerines *(Romanze – Ludwig van Beethoven)*

14. "I Want to Get Married!" *(Für Elise – Ludwig van Beethoven)*

15. The Incredible, Credible Sea *(A Passing Storm – Walter Carroll)*

16. Michael Angelo Bobb *(Concerto No. 1, BWV 1052 – Johann Sebastian Bach)*

17. Toccata In D Minor *(Toccata in D Minor, BWV 565 – Johann Sebastian Bach)*

18. The Bees… The Flowers… The Breeze… *(Piano Concerto No. 1 – Frédéric Chopin)*

19. It's an Onomatopoeic Jungle Out There! *(Les Sauvages – Jean-Phillipe Rameau)*

20. Mr Spock Perms Doctor Who's Hair *(Dance on the Lawn – Dmitri Kabalevsky)*

21. Burn After Reading! *(The Spectre's Waltz – Michelle Lord)*

22. What NOT To Say When You Have Been Invited To Speak At A School Assembly *(Les Barricades Mystérieuses – François Couperin)*

23. Advantageous Advent *(For Unto Us a Child is Born – George Frideric Handel)*

24. The Eve Of The Great Eve *(Sinfonia (Overture) – George Frideric Handel)*

25. Christmas Greetings One And All! *(Christmas Oratorio – Johann Sebastian Bach)*

26. Sleigh Ride *(Sleigh Ride – Michael Bobb)*

27. Come, Emmanuel, Meet Us *(Voluntary – Michael Bobb)*

28. The Alternative Three Wise Men *(Lullaby Carol (Polish))*

29. Today Is Twelfth Night! *(Scherzo – Dmitri Kabalevsky)*

30. Torn! *(The Trumpet Shall Sound – George Frideric Handel)*

31. God Has Decided *(Wachet Auf, BWV 140 – Johann Sebastian Bach)*

32. Tongues *(Symphony No. 5 – Ludwig van Beethoven)*

33. Here The Deities Approve *(Tango – Igor Strawinsky)*

34. Alberich *(Ride of the Valkyries – Richard Wagner)*